Memories of Green

poems by

Erin Ganaway

Finishing Line Press
Georgetown, Kentucky

Memories of Green
Poems

Copyright © 2017 by Erin Ganaway
ISBN 978-1-63534-299-4 First Edition
All rights reserved under International and Pan-American Copyright Conventions.
No part of this book may be reproduced in any manner whatsoever without written permission from the publisher, except in the case of brief quotations embodied in critical articles and reviews.

ACKNOWLEDGMENTS

Special thanks to the editors of *The Hollins Critic* for their inclusion of "May."

Publisher: Leah Maines

Editor: Christen Kincaid

Cover Art: Greg Turco

Author Photo: Herbert Kuper

Cover Design: Elizabeth Maines McCleavy

Printed in the USA on acid-free paper.
Order online: www.finishinglinepress.com
also available on amazon.com

Author inquiries and mail orders:
Finishing Line Press
P. O. Box 1626
Georgetown, Kentucky 40324
U. S. A.

Table of Contents

Preface

FALL
Bound North 2
Unsung Song 3
Fading 4
Skeleton 5
Thanksgiving 6

WINTER
Memories of Green 8
Buzzard 9
Crossing 10
Hemlock 11
Snow Day 12

SPRING
Migraine 14
Crowning 15
Father Song 16
May 17
When We Sing 18

SUMMER
Ants 20
Galloping 21
Waking 22
August 23
Almost 24

In memory of Lou Frierson, Jr.

Preface

In this chapbook, I set out to document in loose sonnets a year I spent living in a cabin on a lively section of the Chestatee River while teaching at the University of North Georgia. I sought to capture the nuanced moods of the surrounding life and landscape. My project was temporarily lost to the buzz of city life when I returned to Atlanta. The white noise of the rapids was replaced by passing traffic, and the contemplative life academia affords seemed momentarily less viable.

Months after my move back to the city, someone I deeply loved took his own life. Suddenly my neglected chapbook crystallized into not just documentation of the mountain landscape and life but of the final months I shared with someone dear to me. Having parted ways with him halfway through my time in the mountains, I often worked through my grief through poems of memory, longing, and loss. Looking back at what I had written, it seemed strangely prophetic. But I never thought our parting would be so permanent. I never thought the day I watched him back down the gravel drive from my cabin would be the last time I saw him on this earth.

I am starting to believe my writing process is somewhat providential in nature. I set out with some expectation or theme in mind, and over time it takes on a life of its own. I realize now all I can do is work with the present moment and preserve it the best I can. The rest will unfold as it will. But here, now, is my gift to someone who parted this world much too early. Days after he met me, he asked if he would end up in one of my books. I hear his laughter as I write these words. And it is as hearty as ever.

EG 2016

FALL

Bound North

Freedom is a passage out of the city,
skyscrapers shrinking in the rearview
mirror. He mixes music for the ride, cranks
down the windows, lights a cigarette.
The highway narrows to a two-lane road,
passing anemic general stores offering
homemade jam and bottled soda, the day
blazing with bespeckled leaves, the tops
of trees fireworked by wind. Kudzu withers
and pastures stubble. This weekend
the hum of bars will give way to dwindling
crickets, the season's last partygoers.
Arriving he asks, *Do you ever not want
something to begin because then it will end?*

Unsung Song

On weekends he brings the brisk
insuck of breeze through the open door,
fleeced greetings, sweet brisket and
local squash from the corner store.
We simmer malbec for thick mugs,
the air outside scented with our
spiced wine, with swept leaves and
skunked galax, as we pick our way
down the gnarled trail to the shallow
pool below the falls. We cup warm
ceramic to nimble our fingers for stone-
skipping, choosing flats of shale
cool and smooth as the autumn evening,
baring its wrists to our unsung song.

Fading

This autumn the leaves
are faded, like ancient
newspaper too frail
to read, the sun casts
sallow on the hillside, and
mist slinks over the river
like a stealthy wraith.

This muted impressionism,
as if seen by aging eyes,
is all rain-doused ochre,
raw umber, vertical
gray—serpentine trees,
lurching and leaning, pale
shadows stretching for light.

Skeleton

The first
   fallen leaf

   is a skeleton
of you, and

your empty
   chair is laced

   in abandoned
webs, ductile

strands that tied
   us viscous,

   those scintillant
threads that once

held us, frail,
   entwined.

Thanksgiving

Somewhere in a haggard motel room, caged
by a wrought iron balcony curved as birthing hips,
two lovers carve each other's names in the air,
their whiskey glasses emptied for the last time.
He can hold both her wrists in one hand,
but her words are grains of sand through his fingers.
In the distance music sighs thinly as her breath,
and the spot-lit shadows of trees lengthen
into a musky night.   Somewhere beyond that
a woman in a thrift faux fur wheels a shopping cart
up and down the sidewalk, muttering something
of this world, something of keeping company
with angels. She says they will only blow smoke
in your mouth, but the stars are miraculous still.

WINTER

Memories of Green

What odds to settle on this stretch of river,
where a rapid once vise-gripped my youth.
Outside this cabin there is always the white
noise of near-death. And it is winter now.
Only the rhododendrons hold memories of green.
I wake each morning to a blink of light
through the window, the north facing silver
sides of trees, a sky like the wet stones
I tasted as a child, when I held the whole earth
in my mouth. There is a cardinal cocking his
head to one side, a request for a bit of seed,
his redness a blood print on this canvas of gray,
his crest pointing upward to you, you who must
have seen me here now, back when I nearly drowned.

Buzzard

The thump of a buzzard woke
me this morning. Landing
outside my bedroom, the mass
of his body a gravestone
grown with lichen, we peered
at one another, I blinked,
and he was gone. I checked my
pulse, and it seems I am still alive.

Now, from the deck, I spot him
circling above, tasting the thermals
for stale blood. Maybe he detects
my loss. He, a shadow on this
glittering day, like a sunspot,
a magnetic disturbance in the core.

Crossing

This has been a long furled winter,
three tanks of propane and a chafed
pocket to keep this cabin thrumming.
I often question why I am here. Maybe
I am here to reclaim that fearless girl,
the one who jumped into the rapids
with no real thought of the outcome.

Today is bright as a newly minted penny
winking from a culvert. The lean pines
wave their arms like variety show
performers on an empty stage. And
I shudder with each fallen branch.
Premature daffodils now bow their heads,
and the rhododendrons hover, expectant.

Hemlock

Under this blanket of winter,
just southeast of the deck,
a hemlock hugs the waist
of a white oak. For months
it held its neighbor's dry leaves
like holiday ornaments, only
to release them to a gust
of early March wind. I see
in the hemlock the green hands
of a compass, not the chalice
of a philosopher's end, but life
embracing life. And with the
scattering of oak leaves, the
brittle hands of time collapsed.

Snow Day

  a heart
     traced
  in snow

  a finger
     numbed
  then
     warmed

  by a mitten
     laundered

  too shrunken
    now
      to hold
  an entire
      hand

SPRING

Migraine

I see wind blowing leaves
through the window

I cannot be a part

I see afternoon grow
white light bright light
through the window

I cannot be a part

I see twilight glow
magic hour soft hour
through the window

I cannot be a part

I see shades drawn low
now cover the window

I am not part

Crowning

This spring there is a slow rise
of dopamine tonguing my skull
like crowning daffodils. All
is amber and champagne-hued.
Light refracts through a wine
glass spinning a webbed prism,
reminding me that soon the
orb weaver will resume his
post at the corner of the deck.
And soon the rhododendrons'
thick fingers will fist into white
plumes. Crows no longer speak
of death—their words fall to bed
like shadows on a passing fog.

Father Song

Last night I fell asleep to a folk song.
Now I can hear the chorus in the river,
the refrain from the wrens. I can still
smell the lacquered wood, the leather
of the guitar strap, as you pulled your
Martin from its case. Four years of age,
I sat pretzel-legged, watching you strum
the chords, washed in the metallic trill,
the lull of your voice. I tucked into bed
in a silken nightgown, frost-pink as this
shroud of blushing rhododendrons,
my heart, a metronome, keeping time
with your words. Listen—all around us
there is this childhood, this scintillant song.

May

The silverbells have now let down
their fine petals, those that
swell and sugar the sip
of tiger swallowtails.
The pale fire of a wild
azalea blazes erect
in stippled sunlight and
the bare limbs of trees
have folded to leaves
lustful and lime. It seems we
are wrought for the churn
of spring and we turn to waltz
when it arrives. We, who
like children, spread our hands wide.

When We Sing

I want to tell you about the deep
sigh of life swelling into this ravine:
the wild and whiling yellow violets,
the lavender asters, the dogwoods
begging to bare their crosses.
I want you to hear the river amplified
by three days of rain, but also the
unflagging murmur of the brook,
southward of the cabin, stretching
its sinewy legs for the east. But truly
your absence is mouth-blown glass,
feeble and reedy as my remembrance
of you, and when we sing—yes all of us
sing—it shatters.

SUMMER

Ants
written with Lou Frierson

nano miles away
    from home

wandering the pale
    pavement alone

when he was a child
    he acted

entered stage left
    a young boy

picking blood red
    from scraped knees

crawling forlorn
    exposed as crushed

mounds scattering
    the distance home

Galloping

In the barn, cement floor cold on my bare soles,
I plunge a hand deep into a barrel of oats just
to feel the silky texture. And in the field I am careful
where I place my feet, because one misstep could
yield a break, fired and fixed iron splintering bones.
I come only with the twine I cut from a bale of hay,
tied into a loop to slide over your neck. Grabbing
fistfuls of mane, I ease myself into the curve
of your back, feel the tickle of fur against my calves.
You step forward, and the twine now seems too brittle
between my fingers. But I tug toward the open
end of the pasture, squeezing with both legs now—
pushing you ahead with a signal I know you will obey,
I have failed to consider the signal I will use to stop.

Waking

He said there are double worlds,
and against crystal a dove will
split into two. But be careful,
he said, for one will be the devil.
The devil comes after the dove,
he said, and temptation comes
in slant form.

                I wake by saying
your name and find your
body crescent-like behind me,
the kindling of your hands
warming me into your world,
where our morning yawns open
like the release of chickweed
petals after the pass of a storm.

August

The air is liquid with remembrance, working
my heart muscles like an undercurrent.
The quick purse of your lips after a smile,
this, a signal for our loving. Eyes like crushed
bottle-glass glinting in the pit of summer,
your hands would rough my hip-bones,
my clavicles, my thighs thumb-printed
and purpling the day after. Sheets snaked
across the floor, I would linger uncovered
in bed, the smoke of your cigarette stealing
into the window with the thick steam of August.

In death you are lean and silent as a candle flame,
carving a space out of the darkness
for one ravaged moment of then, here now.

Almost

Almost erased the lipstick stain on your collar
before returning to dinner. Almost poured
out the last glass of champagne, on a sleepless
night in a jazzy hotel room, to stay up and
see the sunrise bruising the coastal southeast sky.

Almost chose the gown, chapel length lace
light as meringue. Almost chose the date,
the flurried pulse of summer, the breath
of honey and clover—only a mountain
shadow, a phantasm of a life already bleeding.

Almost persuaded you to stay. Almost picked
up the phone the final time you called.

Almost heard your last heartbeat, one faint
whisper from four-hundred-eighty miles away.

Erin Ganaway is the author of a full-length collection of poetry, The *Waiting Girl* (Texas Review Press, 2013), winner of the Texas Review Press Breakthrough Poetry Prize: Georgia. Her poetry has appeared or is forthcoming in many journals and anthologies, including an anthology of poems and photography edited by Georgia Poet Laureate Judson Mitcham, *Inspired Georgia,* as well as *Best New Poets* and *The Southern Poetry Anthology*. She holds a Master of Fine Arts from Hollins University and divides her time between Atlanta and Cape Cod.